Student Workbook 2

Caleb Gattegno

Educational Solutions Worldwide Inc.

Originally published in 1981 as Words in Color Worksheets 8-14.
Republished in 2009.

Educational Solutions Worldwide Inc.
www.EducationalSolutions.com

Table of Contents

Worksheet 8

1. A number of signs in the following columns have the same sound. Show which they are by marking them in the same way (ex. circle, square, line, etc.).

(1) judge	(2) done	(3) walk
general	blood	fall
soldier	does	bald
page	up	smoke
giant	young	smile

How many signs did you mark? _____

2. Can you say whether the sounds for the underlined signs in the following pairs of words are the same (s) or different (d)?

<u>jo</u>hn

<u>jo</u>an
 s, d

f<u>oo</u>d

fl<u>oo</u>d
 s, d

si<u>ng</u>er

fi<u>ng</u>er
 s, d

re<u>a</u>l

f<u>a</u>lse
 s, d

w<u>oo</u>d

c<u>oo</u>l
 s, d

How many are the same? _____

How many are different? _____

4

3. Do you know what each of the following words means? If you
    can, make a drawing for each word.

watch   **string**   **soap**

letter   **walker**   **hook**

page   **giant**   **bird**

cage   **farm**   **roof**

How many words did you illustrate? _____

4. Draw a line under all *s* signs as in *is* and above all those that sound as in *us*.

sings	pets	dolls	birds
sits	things	dads	pups
binds	winds	tops	months
roses	losses	lessons	lions

How many sound as in *is*? _____

How many sound as in *us*? _____

5. Draw a line under all *th* signs as in *this* and above all those that
    sound as in *thin*.

with   month   north   think

than   three   seventh   then

without   them   math   within

those   things   filthy   these

How many sound as in *this*? _____

How many sound as in *thin*? _____

6. Draw a line under all *ch* signs as in *church* and above all those that sound as in *chorus*.

orchestra   china   chill   chrome

inch   christmas   choir   ocher

chips   child   orchid   pinch

ache   punch   chest   lunch

How many sound as in *church*? _____

How many sound as in *chorus*? _____

7. Make sentences out of some of these words. You may use
    the *s* to make plurals.

we   to   a   fat   stop   house   do   he   's

is   late   not   has   at   thin   as   s

salt   man   his   does   go   little

and   it   dog   she   tom   left   have

How many have you made? _____

8. Choose 25 words from anywhere in Reading Primers R1, R2 and up to page 6 of R3 and write them here.

Now make sentences out of some of these words.

How many have you made? _____

9. On Table 6.2 in R3 you see new signs. On page 9, you see new signs and some signs you already know. Write down those that correspond to

(1) a new sound.

(2) a sound you already know.

10. Which of these words use any of the signs introduced on Table 6.2?
Draw a line under each word that does use one of the signs, and a line
over each word that does not. If you are not sure, put a ₓ in front of the
word.

swim   blaze   few

zen   conscience   work

field   writing   beet

soil   near   answers

How many lines under? _____

How many lines over? _____

How many ✗'s ? _____

11. Can you write the following sentence, leaving out some words without changing the meaning?

the large black cat got into the small road behind the shop

Write your sentences here.

Now use the words to form new sentences with different meanings.

How many sentences did you write? _____

12. Which of the following sentences can go together and be part of the same story if read one after the other?

1. dad's toes are large

2. most of us like fresh water

3. the path was hard and he got tired

4. the well is full after the storm

5. we can drink now

6. his shoes hurt his left foot more than his right

Which sentence goes with which? (Give the number of the sentences)

_____ _____ _____ _____ _____

_____ _____ _____ _____ _____

_____ _____ _____ _____ _____

_____ _____ _____ _____ _____

13. Which of the following sentences make sense and which do not?

1. he was falling walking   yes no

2. her finger was looking   yes no

3. the ink bottle was full of blood   yes no

4. the soldier told the general off   yes no

5. strong hooks are made of soft wood   yes no

6. the singer rings the bell   yes no

14. Write a story of up to four sentences that includes the following words:

he   sun   wet   not   hot

with   was   in   after

15. **Read story #6 in your Book of Stories and put down the words you understand.**

Write the words you do not understand here.

16.   **Write out more sentences to add to story #6.**

How many have you written? _____

Now add up your scores. This is your total score for Worksheet #8.

Score _____

Date _____

Worksheet 9

1. A number of signs in the following columns have the same sound. Show which they are by marking them in the same way (ex. circle, square, line, etc.).

(1) string   **(2) island**   **(3) vulture**

long   eyes   adventure

among   high   action

falling   aisle   generation

strung   night   fashion

How many signs did you mark? _____

2. Can you say whether the sounds for the underlined signs in the following pairs of words are the same (s) or different (d)?

y<u>ou</u>ng
    s, d
d<u>ou</u>ble

<u>ou</u>r
    s, d
<u>ou</u>t

gr<u>ou</u>p
    s, d
s<u>ou</u>l

m<u>ou</u>se
    s, d
t<u>ou</u>gh

hal<u>f</u>
    s, d
trou<u>gh</u>

How many are the same? _____

How many are different? _____

3. Do you know what each of the following words means?
    If you can, make a drawing for each word.

trout   village   route

four   soup   calf

mouse   cough   friend

house   orange   half

How many words did you illustrate? _____

23

4. In which of the following words does *ou* sound the same? Rewrite those words together.

tough   trough   troupe   courage   double

mouse   hour   your   trouble   four

loud   cough   soul   group

How many groups have you found? _____

5. Do any of the underlined signs in the following rows have the same sound? Re-write the words that make the same sound below.

(1) m<u>au</u>ve l<u>au</u>gh overh<u>au</u>l l<u>au</u>ghing p<u>au</u>l m<u>au</u>l

(2) tr<u>i</u>al pl<u>i</u>able marr<u>ia</u>ge carr<u>ia</u>ge

(3) fr<u>ie</u>nd l<u>ie</u> f<u>ie</u>ld rel<u>ie</u>f p<u>ie</u>

(4) fie<u>ld</u> wou<u>ld</u> cou<u>ld</u> shou<u>ld</u> shie<u>ld</u>

How many groups have you found?   (1) _____
                                   (2) _____
                                   (3) _____
                                   (4) _____

6. Put a line below the signs *ed* that sound as in *finished* and above them if they sound as in *rolled*.

wedded   married   stopped   backed

rented   hired   linked   salted

punched   robbed   cluttered   polished

stoned   priced   pegged   surfed

How many sound as in *finished*? _____

How many sound as in *rolled*? _____

7. Make sentences out of some of these words. You may use the *s* to make plurals.

came	at	none	sun	on	in	one	he
pat	not	just	be	did	day	lots	ran
's	s	every	and	yet	was	into	more
well	do	I	been	tom	are	as	sam
has	the	store	big	have	school	will	fast

How many have you made? _____

8.   Choose 25 words from anywhere in Reading Primers R1, R2 and up to page 18 of R3 and write them here.

Now make sentences out of some of these words.

How many sentences you made? _____

9. On Table 6.5 in R₃ you see new signs. On page 21, you see new signs and some signs you already know. Write down those that correspond to

(1) a new sound.

(2) a sound you already know.

10. Which of these words use any of the signs introduced on Table 6.5?
    Draw a line under each word that does use one of the signs, and a line
    over each word that does not. If you are not sure, put a ✗ in front of
    the word.

honesty   when   how   zero   antique

cane   captain   hi   oil   hear

cough   hare   tight   hour   island

How many lines under? _____

How many lines over? _____

How many ✗'s? _____

11. Can you write the following sentence, leaving out some words without changing the meaning?

I paid too much money for a brand new leather coat with a fur collar

Write your sentences here.

Now use the words to form new sentences with different meanings.

How many sentences have you made? _____

12. Which of the following sentences can go together and be part of the same story if read one after the other?

1. **because it was raining he ran to the door for shelter**

2. **near the curb there was a limousine**

3. **she was a very pretty girl**

4. **the first prize was given to her**

5. **a man came out of the car**

6. **and he asked her to go in**

Which sentence goes with which? (Give the number of the sentences)

_____ _____ _____ _____ _____

_____ _____ _____ _____

_____ _____ _____ _____

_____ _____ _____ _____

13. Which of the following sentences make sense and which do not?

1. my son is a girl   yes no

2. his friend is my friend   yes no

3. all of us sleep at night   yes no

4. a colonel is an old soldier   yes no

5. the car started its flight on the   yes no
   runway

6. what elephant is this tusk   yes no

14. Write a story of up to four sentences that includes the following words:

blue alone sad night travel yesterday still

15. **Read story #10 in your Book of Stories and put down the words you understand**

and those you do not understand.

16. Write out more sentences to add to story #10.

How many have you written? _____

Now add up your scores. This is your total score for Worksheet #9.

Score _____

Date _____

Worksheet 10

1. A number of signs in the following columns have the same sound. Show which they are by marking them in the same way (ex. circle, square, line, etc.).

(1) before	(2) rhythm	(3) mom
door	wrong	lamb
exhaust	colonel	lame
paul	more	common
pour	far	hymn
all	purr	diaphragm

How many signs did you mark? _____

2. Can you say whether the sounds for the underlined signs in the following pairs of words are the same (s) or different (d)?

<u>s</u>ame
s, d
<u>z</u>ebra

<u>kn</u>ow
s, d
fro<u>n</u>t

p<u>au</u>l
s, d
m<u>au</u>ve

<u>c</u>ake
s, d
a<u>ch</u>e

hal<u>v</u>es
s, d
se<u>v</u>en

How many are the same? _____

How many are different? _____

3. Do you know what each of the following words means? If you can, make a drawing for each word.

zinc   buoy   field

bull   married   calves

lettuce   oil   pie

bazaar   light   luggage

How many words did you illustrate? _____

4. Find words in each column that share a sound. Re-write the words
    next to each other below.

(1)	(2)	(3)
married	field	shoes
belief	mold	does
rye	mild	roes
yield	pound	goes
sigh	would	people

How many groups have you found? _____

5. Write the words in the following lists together if you think that the underlined signs in them sound the same.

(1)   f<u>ew</u>   n<u>ew</u>   s<u>ew</u>age   s<u>ew</u>n   j<u>ew</u>elry

(2)   tiss<u>ue</u>   t<u>ue</u>sday   p<u>ew</u>   tr<u>ue</u>   cr<u>ue</u>l

(3)   ru<u>ss</u>ian   <u>s</u>ugar   <u>sh</u>op   na<u>ti</u>on   que<u>sti</u>on

(4)   <u>g</u>ame   <u>g</u>uard   a<u>ge</u>   <u>gh</u>ost   tou<u>gh</u>

How many groups have you found?   (1) _____
                                     (2) _____
                                     (3) _____
                                     (4) _____

6. Put a line below the signs *ey* that sound as in *valley* and one above those that sound as *ay* in *ray*.

valley   ray   play   mayor

prey   monday   prayers   railway

money   away   sunday   players

friday   trolley   volley   they

How many sound as in *valley*? _____

How many sound as in *ray*? _____

7. Make sentences out of some of these words. You may use the s to make plurals.

see	he	who	are	and	hard
not	write	train	in	on	the
it	jim	house	when	at	is
a	blind	not	s	's	before
because	can	paul			

How many have you made? _____

8.   **Choose 25 words from anywhere in Reading Primers R1, R2 and up to page 25 of R3 and write them here.**

Now make sentences out of some of these words.

How many have you made? _____

9. On Table 7.2 in R3 you see new signs. On page 31 you see new signs and some signs you already know. Write down those that correspond to

(i) a new sound.

(ii) a sound you already know.

10. Which of these words use any of the signs introduced on Table 7.2?
    Draw a line under each word that does use one of the signs, and a
    line over each word that does not.
    If you are not sure, put a **✗** in front of the word.

said   true   thought   guard   dough

not   sewn   when   pants   paw

see   below   would   shoe   couldn't

How many lines under? _____

How many lines over? _____

How many **✗**'s ? _____

11. Can you re-write the following sentence, leaving out some words without changing the meaning?

as he left his home at the top of the hill he was caught in a very bad storm

Write your sentences here.

Now use the words to form new sentences with different meanings.

How many sentences did you make? _____

12. Which of the following sentences can go together and be part of the same story if read one after the other?

1. his camera was loaded with color film

2. the mountains were so beautiful in the sunlight

3. john was a very daring young man

4. the wild animal moved gracefully among the rocks

5. in his eyes there was no fear

6. he took two shots

Which sentence goes with which? (Give the number of the sentences)

_____ _____ _____ _____ _____

_____ _____ _____ _____ _____

_____ _____ _____ _____ _____

_____ _____ _____ _____ _____

13.   Which of the following sentences make sense and which do not?

1. when the sun is out it is night time   yes   no

2. I can see the moon during the day   yes   no

3. people wear their shirts under their vests   yes   no

4. flat shoes have high heels   yes   no

5. people become fat by not eating   yes   no

6. the green grass became brown in the drought   yes   no

14. Write a story of up to four sentences that includes the following words:

reed   boat   swim   river   ocean   where   sunset

15. **Read story #13 in your Book of Stories and put down the words you understand**

and those you do not understand.

16. Write out more sentences to add to story #13.

How many have you written? _____

Now add up your scores. This is your total score for Worksheet #10.

Score _____

Date _____

Worksheet 11

1. A number of signs in the following columns have the same sound.
    Show which they are by marking them in the same way.

(1) who	(2) there	(3) fruit
while	mare	cool
whether	air	put
whose	rail	suit
where	heir	suite

How many signs did you mark? _____

2. Can you say whether the sounds for the underlined signs in the following pairs of words are the same (s) or different (d)?

w<u>o</u>m<u>e</u>n
capt<u>ai</u>n   **s, d**

<u>h</u>e<u>ir</u>
p<u>air</u>   **s, d**

<u>wh</u>ite
<u>wh</u>o   **s, d**

b<u>u</u>sy
b<u>u</u>ry   **s, d**

p<u>ai</u>d
s<u>ai</u>d   **s, d**

How many are the same? _____

How many are different? _____

3.   Do you know what each of the following words means? If you can, make a drawing for each word.

muzzle   **nail**   **saddle**

sword   **fruit**   **sieve**

knee   **lamb**   **rain**

buzz   **mare**   **suit**

How many drawings did you make? _____

4. Which of the following words make the same sound for the same sign? Which do not? Write the words that use the same sign for the same sound next to each other.

<u>c</u>at	li<u>st</u>	thu<u>mb</u>
ba<u>ck</u>	la<u>st</u>	tu<u>mb</u>ler
<u>c</u>ell	lo<u>st</u>	la<u>mb</u>
<u>s</u>ell	fa<u>st</u>en	ru<u>mb</u>ler
<u>c</u>ello	li<u>st</u>en	du<u>mb</u>

How many words have you grouped? _____

5. Write the words of the following lists together if you think that the underlined signs in them sound the same.

(1) s<u>ea</u>   h<u>ea</u>ven   spr<u>ea</u>d   thr<u>ea</u>d   w<u>ea</u>k   p<u>ea</u>r

(2) m<u>ai</u>l   m<u>ai</u>ntain   s<u>ai</u>d   <u>ai</u>r   p<u>ai</u>d   th<u>e</u>re

(3) pier<u>ce</u>   <u>c</u>inema   <u>c</u>on<u>ce</u>ive   <u>c</u>ry   <u>c</u>ell   <u>s</u>even

(4) <u>you</u>th   <u>u</u>se   <u>u</u>nited   <u>ewe</u>   <u>view</u>   <u>u</u>ntil

How many groups have you found?   (1) _____

(2) _____

(3) _____

(4) _____

6. Put a line below the signs that sound as *ea* in *pear* and one above those that sound as in *tea*.

heart	earl	weather	seal
break	mean	pearl	near
lead	heaven	great	weak
sea	thread	lean	year

How many sound as in *pear*? _____

How many sound as in *tea*? _____

7.   Make sentences out of some of these words. You may use the *s* to make plurals.

has	had	it	other	road	a	at
's	man	was	car	in	cat	killed
by	s	saved	not	on	be	said
day	woman	stop	were	the	will	

How many have you made? _____

8. Choose 25 words from anywhere in Reading Primers R1, R2 and up to page 38 of R3 and write them here.

Now make sentences out of some of these words.

How many have you made? _____

9.   In Table 7.4 of R₃ you see new signs. On page 41 you see new signs and some signs you already know. Write down those that correspond to

(1) a new sound.

(2) a sound you already know.

10. Which of these words use any of the signs introduced on Table 7.4?
    Draw a line under each word that does use one of the signs, and a
    line over each word that does not.
    If you are not sure, put a ✗ in front of the word.

sergeant   ache   once   any   anxious

bury   buzz   boy   suite   psalm

tongue   sword   lead   guest   pneumonia

How many lines under? _____

How many lines over? _____

How many ✗'s ? _____

11. Can you re-write the following sentence, leaving out some words without changing the meaning?

the very old man told the whole family he would not live for very much longer and that every penny he had was to be kept for all of them

Write your sentences here.

Now use the words to form new sentences with different meanings.

How many answers have you got? _____

.

12. Which of the following sentences can go together and be part of the same story if read one after the other?

1. he is the last child in the family

2. mother likes to give him the best she has

3. at the age of eight

4. no one would believe it but

5. he eats well and grows fast

6. he does not yet go to school

Which sentence goes with which? (Give the number of the sentences)

_____ _____ _____ _____ _____

_____ _____ _____ _____ _____

_____ _____ _____ _____ _____

_____ _____ _____ _____ _____

13. Which of the following sentences make sense and which do not?

1. he was so afraid that he smiled happily   yes   no

2. his uncle is also my uncle   yes   no

3. every father is also the son of someone   yes   no

4. there are seeds in every orange   yes   no

5. his car runs without an engine   yes   no

6. I can write blue with white chalk   yes   no

14. Write a story of up to four sentences that includes the following words:

soldier captain journey desert little fast gun

15. **Read story #17 in your Book of Stories and put down the words you understand**

and those you do not understand.

16. Write out more sentences to add to story #17.

How many have you written? _____

Now add up your scores. This is your total score for Worksheet #11.

Score _____

Date _____

Worksheet 12

1. A number of signs in the following columns have the same sound.
    Show which they are by marking them in the same way.

(1) weather	(2) height	(3) sign
whether	freight	signal
where	fright	align
here	eighty	spine
near	mighty	

How many have sounds have you marked? _____

2. Can you say whether the sounds for the underlined signs in the following pairs of words are the same (s) or different (d)?

gr<u>ea</u>t
           s, d
str<u>aig</u>ht

n<u>ough</u>t
           s, d
c<u>aug</u>ht

sci<u>ss</u>ors
           s, d
mu<u>sc</u>le

<u>ow</u>l
           s, d
h<u>air</u>

f<u>our</u>
           s, d
s<u>our</u>

How many are the same? _____

How many are different? _____

3. Do you know what each of the following words means? If you can, make a drawing for each word.

people   **ocean**   **scythe**

one   **garage**   **owl**

machine   **pearl**   **muscle**

sign   **diaphragm**   **ear**

How many drawings did you make? _____

4. Which words in the following lists have a sound in common?
   Re-write those words together below.

(1)	(2)	(3)
anxious	pneumonia	cigarette
anxiety	wednesday	thyme
taxi	pneumatic	receipt
examination	known	debtor
xylophone	knee	yacht

How many groups have you found? _____

5. Write words from the following lists together if you think that the underlined signs in them sound the same.

(1) sci<u>ss</u>ors   po<u>ss</u>ess   bu<u>s</u>y   schi<u>sm</u>   wi<u>se</u>   va<u>st</u>

(2) <u>sc</u>ent   mu<u>sc</u>le   <u>s</u>low   <u>c</u>yst   e<u>x</u>it   clo<u>thes</u>

(3) d<u>au</u>ghter   <u>a</u>ll   f<u>or</u>   c<u>au</u>se   <u>ough</u>t   w<u>a</u>s

(4) <u>ps</u>yche   <u>ps</u>alms   <u>s</u>almon   <u>sc</u>ience   an<u>sw</u>er   servi<u>ce</u>

How many groups have you found?   (1) _____

   (2) _____

   (3) _____

   (4) _____

6. Draw a line below the signs that sound as *ough* in *though* and one above those that sound as in *thought*.

bough   nought   brought   borough

through   although   bought   ought

dough   slow   fought   thorough

How many sound as in *though*? _____

How many sound as in *thought*? _____

7. Make sentences out of some of these words. You may use the *s* to make plurals.

coming	still	away	now	this	tunnel	was
which	later	not	he	's	age	is
she	of	looked	s	him	that	tell
through	the	home	yet	at		

How many have you made? _____

8. Choose 25 words from anywhere in Reading Primers R1, R2 and up to page 53 in R3 and write them here.

Now make sentences out of some of these words.

How many have you made? _____

9.   In Table 7.8 in R3 you see new signs. On page 59 you see new signs and some signs you already know. Write down those that correspond to

(1) a new sound.

(2) a sound you already know.

10. Which of these words use any of the signs introduced on Table 7.8?
    Draw a line under each word that does use one of the signs, and a
    line over each word that does not.
    If you are not sure, put a **✗** in front of the word.

daughter   **island**   **foreign**   **review**

pizza   **conscience** **knowledge** **adieu**

ear   **myth**   **straight**   **amoeba**

How many lines under? _____

How many lines over? _____

How many ✗'s ? _____

11. Can you write the following sentence, leaving out some words without changing the meaning?

as the journey was long the people in the coach became very friendly and talked about all sorts of things while looking through the windows at the changing landscape

Write your sentences here.

Now use the words to form new sentences with different meanings.

How many sentences have you made? _____

12. Which of the following sentences can go together and be part of the same story if read one after the other?

1. the cowboy had one gun in each hand

2. on the horizon one could see the house and the smoking chimney

3. the horses were tied near the entrance

4. after traveling for a few days he was not far from home

5. inside the family was waiting

6. nobody noticed anything

Which sentence goes with which? (Give the number of the sentences)

_____ _____ _____ _____ _____

_____ _____ _____ _____ _____

_____ _____ _____ _____ _____

_____ _____ _____ _____ _____

13. Which of the following sentences make sense and which do not?

1. he can walk on his hands   yes   no

2. the car reversed into the garage   yes   no

3. this man can see stars during the day   yes   no

4. she talks and walks in her sleep   yes   no

5. tomorrow is another day   yes   no

6. when one is old one is no longer young   yes   no

14. Write a story of up to four sentences that includes the following
    words:

straight   orchestra   music   hall   visit   abroad   now

15. **Read story #20 in your Book of Stories and put down the words you understand**

and those you do not understand.

16. Write out more sentences to add to story #20.

How many have you written? _____

Now add up your scores. This is your total score for Worksheet #12.

Score _____

Date _____

Worksheet 13

1. **Read story #10 in the Book of Stories. Then answer the following questions.**

   i. who is aunt rachel?

   ii. how old is she?

   iii. what does aunt rachel do at home?

   iv. name a few of the garments she has embroidered

   v. why does aunt rachel not visit the girls at home?

2.   **Read story #11 in the Book of Stories. Then answer the following questions.**

i.   **why did tim wake up in the night?**

ii.   **what did mom do to him?**

iii.   **what did dad say to her about tim?**

iv.   **what did tim dream of?**

v.   **what did sam say dreams were?**

vi.   **do you ever dream?**   **what about?**

3. Read story #13 in the Book of Stories. Then answer the following questions.

    i.   who is miss dunn?

    ii. which lessons does pam like best?

    iii. what instruments does miss dunn play?

    iv. what do other pupils do when one of them is asked to sing?

    v.   what is the game that the pupils love?

    vi. what does mom suggest her children should do?

4. Read story #14 in the Book of Stories. Then answer the following questions.

    i.   what was mom doing in the kitchen?

    ii. what did she answer sam when he asked if he could help?

    iii. how does sam say he could prepare the eggs?

    iv. how does he think he can prepare french dressing?

    v.   what did mom tell pam and pat?

    vi. who do you think is meaner, sam or pat and pam?

5. Read story #15 in the Book of Stories. Then answer the following questions.

    i.   where did dad take tim?   why?

    ii.   what did tim want to know?

    iii. what did the salesperson ask tim?

    iv. what did dad tell the salesperson?

    v.   what did dad tell tim?

    vi. what did tim think to himself?

6. Read story #17 in the Book of Stories. Then answer the following questions.

i.   why would mother call them in?

ii.   what would be on the table?

iii.   which are the dishes disliked by each of the children?

iv.   what does sam eat when he gets what he does not like?

v.   which is the meal they all like?

vi.   why can't mom give it to them every day?

7. Read story #18 in the Book of Stories. Then answer the following
    questions.

    i.   what was brought in from the truck?

    ii. what did mom answer the children who wanted to open the
         box?

    iii. what did the children think was inside?

    iv. how did they make sure that their guesses were right or wrong?

    v.   what did dad do on arrival?

    vi. what did the children bring out of the box?   how did they get
         it out?

8. Read story #19 in the Book of Stories. Then answer the following questions.

   i. what did pam think when she saw pat looking into the bucket?

   ii. what did the children look at?

   iii. what did dad suggest to them?

   iv. what happened when the drops fell faster and faster?

   v. when the bucket was slightly moved what happened?

   vi. what did dad tell them to do?

9. Read story #21 in the Book of Stories. Then answer the following questions.

    i.   how did dad's story start?

    ii. what was the gift of the fairy?

    iii. how did the king and queen try to find out what the gift was?

    iv. where did the king take vilnan and for what?

    v.   what did vilnan answer the people?

    vi. what is it to have eyes like vilnan?

10. Read story #25 in the Book of Stories. Then answer the following questions.

    i.   what happened in the train?

    ii. what did they see in the fields?

    iii. what did they have to eat and drink?

    iv. what did sam do during the journey?

    v. who was waiting at the station?

    vi. what did the man do and say?

11. Read story #28 in the Book of Stories. Then answer the following questions.

    i. what did pam and pat want to do?

    ii. what did they ask mom?

    iii. what did they say to the salesperson?

    iv. what did the salesperson do?

    v. what happened about needles?

    vi. what did they start knitting?

12. **Read story #30 in the Book of Stories. Then answer the following questions.**

    i.   where did the children go?

    ii.   what was the water they drank like?

    iii. what was the mill like from outside?

    iv. what did the miller explain to the children?

    v.   who owned the mill in the past?

    vi. what did the miller say about his dog?

13. **Read story #32 in the Book of Stories. Then answer the following questions.**

   i. what happened to pat to have her foot put in a cast?

   ii. what did the doctor do?

   iii. where did pat spend a few days?   for how long?

   iv. what were her feelings?

   v. when was everything normal again?

   vi. what did pat forget then?

14. **Read story #33 in the Book of Stories. Then answer the following questions.**

   i.   where did the three children go?

   ii. can you write a few words about the place as the children found it?

   iii. why did sam tell them to turn back?

   iv. why was tom sorry?

   v.   what did they do when they came out?

   vi. what did they think about their next visit?

15. **Read story #34 in your Book of Stories. Then answer the following questions.**

    i.   where were sam and tom?

    ii.   what was the time?

    iii. what did they look at?

    iv. what did sam say?

    v.   what did tom think?

    vi. what did they feel about the sky?

16. **Read story #37 in your Book of Stories. Then answer the following questions.**

    i.   what did Pam ask Mom for?

    ii.   why was it not so easy to give Pam what she wanted?

    iii.   what did Mom say that pleased Pam and Sam?

    iv.   what did Pam do in Mom's room?

    v.   how did she learn what it is to be alone?

    vi.   how did Mom know that it was right for Pam to be alone?

Now add up your scores. This is your total score for Worksheet #13.

Score _____

Date _____

Worksheet 14

1.   **Which of the following sentences are in the present tense?**

We have a tent in the garden.   yes   no

Sam has many books and likes to read late.   yes   no

When it is warm, we may sleep in the tent.   yes   no

Dad tells us stories, in the house, in the tent, or on the   yes   no
sand.

Mom often asks Pam and Sam to clean the house with   yes   no
her.

A red apple from the top rolled down and fell in the   yes   no
gutter.

2.   Which of the following sentences are in the past tense?

Tim looked at him with his eyes wide open and soon   yes   no
started crying.

When they reached home Tim was still crying.   yes   no

If I had given you one, you would have eaten two and I   yes   no
one.

Tim was puzzled and stopped crying. He could not   yes   no
understand what Sam was saying nor why.

Be careful of the water or open your umbrella.   yes   no

On his way he stopped at a site where a man was   yes   no
working.

3.   Which of the following sentences are in the future tense?

I am sorry to have bothered you. I'll send him with his   yes   no
mother tomorrow.

We should be careful not to let them go to bed too soon   yes   no
after a big dinner.

I hope that you will not drive your mother as crazy as you   yes   no
do me.

First I shall find out which pair I am replacing.   yes   no

Can we open the box now?   yes   no

You must be very careful otherwise you may cut it.   yes   no

4.   Which of the following sentences are conditional?

If I had given you one, you would have eaten two and I   yes   no
one.

Sam looked at his arms and thought: I would like to be as   yes   no
strong as he and have a pneumatic drill to handle.

Why did you go to look for him, when he knew the way   yes   no
home?

Mom knew that they could do nothing now to make Tim   yes   no
not dream.

He would show him the next day that he too could be   yes   no
tough.

Miss Dunn would be pleased if she knew.   yes   no

5. Which of the following sentences are affirmative (a) and which are negative (n) ?

The children are at school five days a week.   a   n

Sam does not play with Tom when he is at school.   a   n

We shall do it together when we have finished what we   a   n
are doing.

I do not mind but you certainly are mean.   a   n

I do not want to have two black pairs or two brown pairs.   a   n

Both pairs were no longer good.   a   n

Tim has not yet made up his mind about the color.   a   n

6. Which of the following sentences are interrogative?

Do you know how to prepare a french dressing salad?	yes	no
Which pair am I replacing?	yes	no
Keep quiet, don't you see that I am trying to put her to sleep?	yes	no
She must have a change even if one or two do not eat what she gives them.	yes	no
Can't you open it and let us see?	yes	no
They all stopped talking about whether it was possible.	yes	no
He asked them whether they would like to make an experiment.	yes	no

7. Which of the following sentences have direct object (d) or an indirect object (i)?

Under the tap there was a bucket and water was slowly   d   i
dripping into it.

I would prefer sugar cane to toothpaste to keep my teeth   d   i
healthy.

Mom and Dad have a friend who is a dentist. His name is   d   i
Mister Brown.

The five children sat on the rug by the armchair in which   d   i
Dad was sitting, waiting for them.

He loves books and especially travel stories.   d   i

Dad showed a map to the children and explained how   d   i
they will go there in two weeks' time.

8.   Which of the following sentences contain more than one clause?

The journey to the vacation home was long and tiring but   yes   no
nothing special happened on the way.

First by car to the station, then by train for three and a half   yes   no
hours, then by car, to the house; in all, five hours' journey.

Tim slept all the time in the train and did not see the many   yes   no
tunnels that they went through.

When he returned to the house breakfast was ready.   yes   no

They had to put their slippers out there so they could   yes   no
change when coming and going.

9.   Change each of the following sentences into the plural.

He ate with good appetite and had two fresh eggs with toast.

Each in turn drank from the dipper and expressed his pleasure at the freshness of the water.

The miller answered that he could grind all the grain in his own fields in one day.

10.   Change each of the following sentences into the present tense.

She found that everybody was right but told them that since they had been so happy in that place perhaps they would return there the following year.

She cried and screamed and called for her mother.

When he took a step forward, the ground went down steeply and the water rose to his knees.

11.   Are there stories in your Book of Stories that are told:

1. in the present tense?   (give the numbers)

2. in the past tense?   (give the numbers)

3. in the first person plural?   (give the numbers)

4. by a narrator?   (give the numbers)

12. Take one of the stories told in the first person plural and see if you can tell it as if you were the narrator. On one side put one or more sentences of the story and your new version on the other.

13.   What do you like about:

Sam?

Pam?

Tom?

Pat?

Tim?

14. **Which of the stories do you like best? Give their numbers and in a few words tell why you like them.**

15. Do you collect postage stamps? Give the names of a few countries from which you have stamps.

Would you like to collect stamps?   Why?

Do you know the difference between a state, country, and a continent? Give examples of each.

16. Go over your worksheets and find out if you can add to some of them and increase your score now.

Worksheet #	Old Score	New Score
1.		
2.		
3.		
4.		
5.		
6.		
7.		
8.		
9.		
10.		
11.		
12.		
13.		
14.		

Now add up your scores. This is your total score for Worksheet #14.

Score _____

Date _____

www.ingramcontent.com/pod-product-compliance
Lightning Source LLC
Chambersburg PA
CBHW080935040426
42443CB00015B/3423